Dear Reader—

You hold in your hands the first title from A Book Apart. Creating brief books for people who make websites has been a dream of ours for years. But turning that dream into a reality took the right combination of partners, and especially the right author and title.

The book in your hands is either the proof or the test of a theory: the theory that important web design topics can be addressed with clarity, brevity, and specificity (not to mention a dash of whimsy). We don't publish these books just because we can. We publish them because this kind of book is new and needed.

We hope you like *HTML5 for Web Designers*. If you love it, tell a friend. If you don't, tell us: abookapart@gmail.com.

Look for future titles on CSS3, content strategy, responsive web design, and designing for emotion from leading authors Dan Cederholm, Erin Kissane, Ethan Marcotte, Aarron Walter, and Luke Wroblewski, coming soon to a website near you. And thanks again for sharing the dream.

Yours,

Jeffrey Zeldman	Jason Santa Maria	Mandy Brown
Publisher	*Designer*	*Editor*

Jeremy Keith

HTML5 FOR WEB DESIGNERS

Publisher: Jeffrey Zeldman
Designer: Jason Santa Maria
Editor: Mandy Brown
Technical Editor: Ethan Marcotte
Copyeditor: Krista Stevens

ISBN 978-0-9844425-0-8

A Book Apart
New York, New York
http://books.alistapart.com

10 9 8 7 6 5

TABLE OF CONTENTS

FOREWORD

When Mandy Brown, Jason Santa Maria and I formed A Book Apart, one topic burned uppermost in our minds, and there was only one author for the job.

Nothing else, not even "real fonts" or CSS3, has stirred the standards-based design community like the imminent arrival of HTML5. Born out of dissatisfaction with the pacing and politics of the W3C, and conceived for a web of applications (not just documents), this new edition of the web's lingua franca has in equal measure excited, angered, and confused the web design community.

Just as he did with the DOM and JavaScript, Jeremy Keith has a unique ability to illuminate HTML5 and cut straight to what matters to accessible, standards-based designer-developers. And he does it in this book, using only as many words and pictures as are needed.

There are other books about HTML5, and there will be many more. There will be 500 page technical books for application developers, whose needs drove much of HTML5's development. There will be even longer secret books for browser makers, addressing technical challenges that you and I are blessed never to need to think about.

But this is a book for you—you who create web content, who mark up web pages for sense and semantics, and who design accessible interfaces and experiences. Call it your user guide to HTML5. Its goal—one it will share with every title in the forthcoming A Book Apart catalog—is to shed clear light on a tricky subject, and do it fast, so you can get back to work.

—Jeffrey Zeldman

1 A BRIEF HISTORY OF MARKUP

HTML IS THE UNIFYING LANGUAGE of the World Wide Web. Using just the simple tags it contains, the human race has created an astoundingly diverse network of hyperlinked documents, from Amazon, eBay, and Wikipedia, to personal blogs and websites dedicated to cats that look like Hitler.

HTML5 is the latest iteration of this lingua franca. While it is the most ambitious change to our common tongue, this isn't the first time that HTML has been updated. The language has been evolving from the start.

As with the web itself, the HyperText Markup Language was the brainchild of Sir Tim Berners-Lee. In 1991 he wrote a document called "HTML Tags" in which he proposed fewer than two dozen elements that could be used for writing web pages.

Sir Tim didn't come up with the idea of using tags consisting of words between angle brackets; those kinds of tags already existed in the SGML (Standard Generalized Markup Language) format. Rather than inventing a new standard, Sir Tim saw the benefit of building on top of what already existed—a trend that can still be seen in the development of HTML5.

FROM IETF TO W3C: THE ROAD TO HTML 4

There was never any such thing as HTML 1. The first official specification was HTML 2.0, published by the IETF, the Internet Engineering Task Force. Many of the features in this specification were driven by existing implementations. For example, the market-leading Mosaic web browser of 1994 already provided a way for authors to embed images in their documents using an `<img>` tag. The `img` element later appeared in the HTML 2.0 specification.

The role of the IETF was superceded by the W3C, the World Wide Web Consortium, where subsequent iterations of the HTML standard have been published at http://www.w3.org. The latter half of the nineties saw a flurry of revisions to the specification until HTML 4.01 was published in 1999.

At that time, HTML faced its first major turning point.

XHTML 1: HTML AS XML

After HTML 4.01, the next revision to the language was called XHTML 1.0. The X stood for "eXtreme" and web developers were required to cross their arms in an X shape when speaking the letter.

No, not really. The X stood for "eXtensible" and arm crossing was entirely optional.

The content of the XHTML 1.0 specification was identical to that of HTML 4.01. No new elements or attributes were added. The only difference was in the syntax of the language. Whereas HTML allowed authors plenty of freedom in how they wrote their elements and attributes, XHTML required authors to follow the rules of XML, a stricter markup language upon which the W3C was basing most of their technologies.

Having stricter rules wasn't such a bad thing. It encouraged authors to use a single writing style. Whereas previously tags and attributes could be written in uppercase, lowercase, or any combination thereof, a valid XHTML 1.0 document required all tags and attributes to be lowercase.

The publication of XHTML 1.0 coincided with the rise of browser support for CSS. As web designers embraced the emergence of web standards, led by The Web Standards Project, the stricter syntax of XHTML was viewed as a "best practice" way of writing markup.

Then the W3C published XHTML 1.1.

While XHTML 1.0 was simply HTML reformulated as XML, XHTML 1.1 was real, honest-to-goodness XML. That meant it couldn't be served with a mime-type of `text/html`. But if authors published a document with an XML mime-type, then the most popular web browser in the world at the time—Internet Explorer—couldn't render the document.

It seemed as if the W3C were losing touch with the day-to-day reality of publishing on the web.

XHTML 2: OH, WE'RE NOT GONNA TAKE IT!

If Dustin Hoffman's character in *The Graduate* had been a web designer, the W3C would have said one word to him, just one word: XML.

As far as the W3C was concerned, HTML was finished as of version 4. They began working on XHTML 2, designed to lead the web to a bright new XML-based future.

Although the name XHTML 2 sounded very similar to XHTML 1, they couldn't have been more different. Unlike XHTML 1, XHTML 2 wasn't going to be backwards compatible with existing web content or even previous versions of HTML. Instead, it was going to be a pure language, unburdened by the sloppy history of previous specifications.

It was a disaster.

THE SCHISM: WHATWG TF?

A rebellion formed within the W3C. The consortium seemed to be formulating theoretically pure standards unrelated to the needs of web designers. Representatives from Opera, Apple, and Mozilla were unhappy with this direction. They wanted to see more emphasis placed on formats that allowed the creation of web applications.

Things came to a head in a workshop meeting in 2004. Ian Hickson, who was working for Opera Software at the time, proposed the idea of extending HTML to allow the creation of web applications. The proposal was rejected.

The disaffected rebels formed their own group: the Web Hypertext Application Technology Working Group, or WHATWG for short.

FROM WEB APPS 1.0 TO HTML5

From the start, the WHATWG operated quite differently than the W3C. The W3C uses a consensus-based approach: issues are raised, discussed, and voted on. At the WHATWG, issues are also raised and discussed, but the final decision on what goes into a specification rests with the editor. The editor is Ian Hickson.

On the face of it, the W3C process sounds more democratic and fair. In practice, politics and internal bickering can bog down progress. At the WHATWG, where anyone is free to contribute but the editor has the last word, things move at a faster pace. But the editor doesn't quite have absolute power: an invitation-only steering committee can impeach him in the unlikely event of a Strangelove scenario.

Initially, the bulk of the work at the WHATWG was split into two specifications: Web Forms 2.0 and Web Apps 1.0. Both specifications were intended to extend HTML. Over time, they were merged into a single specification called simply HTML5.

REUNIFICATION

While HTML5 was being developed at the WHATWG, the W3C continued working on XHTML 2. It would be inaccurate to say that it was going nowhere fast. It was going nowhere very, very slowly.

In October 2006, Sir Tim Berners-Lee wrote a blog post in which he admitted that the attempt to move the web from HTML to XML just wasn't working. A few months later, the W3C issued a new charter for an HTML Working Group. Rather than start from scratch, they wisely decided that the work of the WHATWG should be used as the basis for any future version of HTML.

All of this stopping and starting led to a somewhat confusing situation. The W3C was simultaneously working on two different, incompatible types of markup: XHTML 2 and HTML 5 (note the space before the number five). Meanwhile a separate organization, the WHATWG, was working on a specification called HTML5 (with no space) that would be used as a basis for one of the W3C specifications!

Any web designers trying to make sense of this situation would have had an easier time deciphering a movie marathon of *Memento*, *Primer*, and the complete works of David Lynch.

XHTML IS DEAD: LONG LIVE XHTML SYNTAX

The fog of confusion began to clear in 2009. The W3C announced that the charter for XHTML 2 would not be renewed. The format had been as good as dead for several years; this announcement was little more than a death certificate.

Strangely, rather than passing unnoticed, the death of XHTML 2 was greeted with some mean-spirited gloating. XML naysayers used the announcement as an opportunity to deride anyone who had ever used XHTML 1—despite the fact that XHTML 1 and XHTML 2 have almost nothing in common.

Meanwhile, authors who had been writing XHTML 1 in order to enforce a stricter writing style became worried that HTML5 would herald a return to sloppy markup.

As you'll soon see, that's not necessarily the case. HTML5 is as sloppy or as strict as you want to make it.

THE TIMELINE OF HTML5

The current state of HTML5 isn't as confusing as it once was, but it still isn't straightforward.

There are two groups working on HTML5. The WHATWG is creating an HTML5 specification using its process of "commit then review." The W3C HTML Working Group is taking that specification and putting it through its process of "review then commit." As you can imagine, it's an uneasy alliance. Still, there seems to finally be some consensus about that pesky "space or no space?" question (it's HTML5 with no space, just in case you were interested).

Perhaps the most confusing issue for web designers dipping their toes into the waters of HTML5 is getting an answer to the question, "when will it be ready?"

In an interview, Ian Hickson mentioned 2022 as the year he expected HTML5 to become a proposed recommendation. What followed was a wave of public outrage from some web designers. They didn't understand what "proposed recommendation" meant, but they knew they didn't have enough fingers to count off the years until 2022.

The outrage was unwarranted. In this case, reaching a status of "proposed recommendation" requires two complete implementations of HTML5. Considering the scope of the specification, this date is incredibly ambitious. After all, browsers don't have the best track record of implementing existing standards. It took Internet Explorer over a decade just to add support for the `abbr` element.

The date that really matters for HTML5 is 2012. That's when the specification is due to become a "candidate recommendation." That's standards-speak for "done and dusted."

But even that date isn't particularly relevant to web designers. What really matters is when browsers start supporting features. We began using parts of CSS 2.1 as soon as browsers started shipping with support for those parts. If we had waited for every browser to completely support CSS 2.1 before we started using any of it, we would still be waiting.

It's no different with HTML5. There won't be a single point in time at which we can declare that the language is ready to use. Instead, we can start using parts of the specification as web browsers support those features.

Remember, HTML5 isn't a completely new language created from scratch. It's an evolutionary rather than revolutionary change in the ongoing story of markup. If you are currently creating websites with any version of HTML, you're already using HTML5.

2 THE DESIGN OF HTML5

THE FRENCH REVOLUTION was an era of extreme political and social change. Revolutionary fervor was applied to time itself. For a brief period, the French Republic introduced a decimal time system, with each day divided into ten hours and each hour divided into one hundred minutes. It was thoroughly logical and clearly superior to the sexagesimal system.

Decimal time was a failure. Nobody used it. The same could be said for XHTML 2. The W3C rediscovered the lesson of post-revolutionary France: changing existing behavior is very, very difficult.

DESIGN PRINCIPLES

Keen to avoid the mistakes of the past, the WHATWG drafted a series of design principles to guide the development of HTML5. One of the key principles is to "Support existing content." That means there's no Year Zero for HTML5.

Where XHTML 2 attempted to sweep aside all that had come before, HTML5 builds upon existing specifications and implementations. Most of HTML 4.01 has survived in HTML5.

Some of the other design principles include "Do not reinvent the wheel," and "Pave the cowpaths," meaning, if there's a widespread way for web designers to accomplish a task—even if it's not necessarily the best way—it should be codified in HTML5. Put another way, "If it ain't broke, don't fix it."

Many of these design principles will be familiar to you if you've ever dabbled in the microformats community (http://microformats.org). The HTML5 community shares the same pragmatic approach to getting a format out there, without worrying too much about theoretical problems.

This attitude is enshrined in the design principle of "Priority of constituencies," which states, "In case of conflict, consider users over authors over implementers over specifiers over theoretical purity."

Ian Hickson has stated on many occasions that browser makers are the real arbiters of what winds up in HTML5. If a browser vendor refuses to support a particular proposal, there's no point in adding that proposal to the specification because then the specification would be fiction. According to the priority of constituencies, we web designers have an even stronger voice. If we refuse to use part of the specification, then the specification is equally fictitious.

KEEPING IT REAL

The creation of HTML5 has been driven by an ongoing internal tension. On the one hand, the specification needs to be powerful enough to support the creation of web applications. On the other hand, HTML5 needs to support existing content, even if most existing content is a complete mess. If the specification strays too far in one direction, it will suffer the same fate as XHTML 2. But if it goes too far in the other direction, the specification will enshrine `<font>` tags and tables for layout because, after all, that's what a huge number of web pages are built with.

It's a delicate balancing act that requires a pragmatic, level-headed approach.

ERROR HANDLING

The HTML5 specification doesn't just declare what browsers should do when they are processing well-formed markup. For the first time, a specification also defines what browsers should do when they are dealing with badly formed documents.

Until now, browser makers have had to individually figure out how to deal with errors. This usually involved reverse engineering whatever the most popular browser was doing—not a very productive use of their time. It would be better for browser makers to implement new features rather than waste their time duplicating the way their competitors handle malformed markup.

Defining error handling in HTML5 is incredibly ambitious. Even if HTML5 had exactly the same elements and attributes as HTML 4.01, with no new features added, defining error handling by 2012 would still be a Sisyphean task.

Error handling might not be of much interest to web designers, especially if we are writing valid, well-formed documents to begin with, but it's very important for browser makers. Whereas previous markup specifications were written for authors, HTML5 is written for authors *and* implementers. Bear that in mind when perusing the specification. It explains why the HTML5 specification is so big and why it seems to have been written with a level of detail normally reserved for trainspotters who enjoy a nice game of chess while indexing their stamp collection.

GIVE IT TO ME STRAIGHT, DOCTYPE

A Document Type Declaration, or doctype for short, has traditionally been used to specify which particular flavor of markup a document is written in.

The doctype for HTML 4.01 looks like this (*line wraps marked »*):

```
<!DOCTYPE HTML PUBLIC »
"-//W3C//DTD HTML 4.01//EN" »
"http://www.w3.org/TR/html4/strict.dtd">
```

Here's the doctype for XHTML 1.0:

```
<!DOCTYPE html PUBLIC »
"-//W3C//DTD XHTML 1.0 Strict //EN" »
"http://www.w3.org/TR/xhtml1/DTD/xhtml1-strict.dtd">
```

They're not very human-readable, but, in their own way, they are simply saying "this document is written in HTML 4.01," or "this document is written in XHTML 1.0."

You might expect the doctype declaring "this document is written in HTML5" would have the number five in it somewhere. It doesn't. The doctype for HTML5 looks like this:

```
<!DOCTYPE html>
```

It's so short that even I can memorize it.

But surely this is madness! Without a version number in the doctype, how will we specify future versions of HTML?

When I first saw the doctype for HTML5, I thought it was the height of arrogance. I asked myself, "Do they really believe that this will be the final markup specification ever written?"

It seemed to be a textbook case of Year Zero thinking.

In fact, though, the doctype for HTML5 is very pragmatic. Because HTML5 needs to support existing content, the doctype could be applied to an existing HTML 4.01 or XHTML 1.0 document. Any future versions of HTML will also need to support the existing content in HTML5, so the very concept of applying version numbers to markup documents is flawed.

The truth is that doctypes aren't even important. Let's say you serve up a document with a doctype for HTML 4.01. If that document includes an element from another specification, such as HTML 3.2 or HTML5, a browser will still render that part of the document. Browsers support features, not doctypes.

Document Type Declarations were intended for validators, not browsers. The only time that a browser pays any attention to a doctype is when it is performing "doctype switching"—a clever little hack that switches rendering between quirks mode and standards mode depending on the presence of a decent doctype.

The minimum information required to ensure that a browser renders using standards mode is the HTML5 doctype. In fact, that's the only reason to include the doctype at all. An HTML document written without the HTML5 doctype can still be valid HTML5.

KEEPING IT SIMPLE

The doctype isn't the only thing that has been simplified in HTML5.

If you want to specify the character encoding of a markup document, the best way is to ensure that your server sends the correct `Content-Type` header. If you want to be doubly certain, you can also specify the character set using a `<meta>` tag. Here's the `meta` declaration for a document written in HTML 4.01:

```
<meta http-equiv="Content-Type" content="text/html; »
charset=UTF-8">
```

Here's the much more memorable way of doing the same thing in HTML5:

```
<meta charset="UTF-8">
```

As with the doctype, this simplified character encoding contains the minimum number of characters needed to be interpreted by browsers.

The `<script>` tag is another place that can afford to shed some fat. It's common practice to add a `type` attribute with a value of "text/javascript" to `script` elements:

```
<script type="text/javascript" src="file.js"></script>
```

Browsers don't need that attribute. They will assume that the script is written in JavaScript, the most popular scripting language on the web (let's be honest: the *only* scripting language on the web):

```
<script src="file.js"></script>
```

Likewise, you don't need to specify a `type` value of "text/css" every time you link to a CSS file:

```
<link rel="stylesheet" type="text/css" href="file.css">
```

You can simply write:

```
<link rel="stylesheet" href="file.css">
```

SYNTAX: MARKING IT UP YOUR WAY

Some programming languages, such as Python, enforce a particular way of writing instructions. Using spaces to indent code is mandatory—the white space is significant. Other programming languages, such as JavaScript, don't pay any attention to formatting—the white space at the start of a line isn't significant.

If you're looking for a cheap evening's entertainment, get an array of programmers into the same room and utter the words "significant white space." You can then spend hours warming yourself by the ensuing flame war.

There's a fundamental philosophical question at the heart of the significant white space debate: should a language enforce a particular style of writing, or should authors be free to write in whatever style they like?

Markup doesn't require significant white space. If you want to add a new line and an indentation every time you nest an element, you can do so, but browsers and validators don't require it. This doesn't mean that markup is a free-for-all. Some flavors of markup enforce a stricter writing style than others.

Before XHTML 1.0, it didn't matter if you wrote tags in uppercase or lowercase. It didn't matter whether or not you quoted attributes. For some elements, it didn't even matter whether you included the closing tag.

XHTML 1.0 enforces the syntax of XML. All tags must be written in lowercase. All attributes must be quoted. All elements must have a closing tag. In the special case of standalone elements such as `br`, the requirement for a closing tag is replaced with a requirement for a closing slash: `<br />`.

With HTML5, anything goes. Uppercase, lowercase, quoted, unquoted, self-closing or not; it's entirely up to you.

I've been using the XHTML 1.0 doctype for years. I like the fact that I must write in one particular style and I like the way that the W3C validator enforces that style. Now that I'm using HTML5, it's up to me to enforce the style I want.

I can see why some people don't like the looseness of the HTML5 syntax. It seems like it's turning the clock back on years of best practices. Some people have even said that the lax syntax of HTML5 is encouraging bad markup. I don't think that's true, but I can see why it's a concern. It's as if a programming language that enforced significant white space suddenly changed over to a more forgiving rule set.

Personally, I'm okay with the casual syntax of HTML5. I've come to terms with having to enforce my own preferred writing style myself. But I would like to see more tools that would allow me to test my markup against a particular style. In the world of programming, these are called lint tools: programs that flag up suspect coding practices. A lint tool for markup would be different than a validator, which checks against a doctype; but it would be wonderful if the two could be combined into one lean, mean validating linting machine.

Whosoever shall program such a device will earn the undying respect and admiration of web designers everywhere.

WE DON'T USE THAT KIND OF LANGUAGE

In past versions of HTML, whenever a previously existing element or attribute was removed from the specification, the process was called deprecation. Web designers were advised not to use deprecated elements, or send them Christmas cards, or even mention them in polite company.

There are no deprecated elements or attributes in HTML5. But there are plenty of *obsolete* elements and attributes.

No, this isn't a case of political correctness gone mad. "Obsolete" has a subtly different meaning from "deprecated."

Because HTML5 aims to be backwards compatible with existing content, the specification must acknowledge previously existing elements even when those elements are no longer in HTML5. This leads to a slightly confusing situation where the specification simultaneously says, "authors, don't use this element" and, "browsers, here's how you should render this element." If the element were deprecated, it wouldn't be mentioned in the specification at all; but because the element is obsolete, it is included for the benefit of browsers.

Unless you're building a browser, you can treat obsolete elements and attributes the same way you would treat deprecated elements and attributes: don't use them in your web pages and don't invite them to cocktail parties.

If you insist on using an obsolete element or attribute, your document will be "non-conforming." Browsers will render everything just fine, but you might hear a tut-ing sound from the website next door.

So long, been good to know ya

The `frame`, `frameset`, and `noframes` elements are obsolete. They won't be missed.

The `acronym` element is obsolete, thereby freeing up years of debating time that can be better spent calculating the angel-density capacity of standard-sized pinheads. Do not mourn the `acronym` element; just use the `abbr` element instead. Yes, I know there's a difference between acronyms and abbreviations—acronyms are spoken as single words, like NATO and SCUBA—but just remember: all acronyms are abbreviations, but not all abbreviations are acronyms.

Presentational elements such as `font`, `big`, `center`, and `strike` are obsolete in HTML5. In reality, they've been obsolete for years; it's much easier to achieve the same presentational effects using CSS properties such as `font-size` and `text-align`. Similarly, presentational attributes such as `bgcolor`, `cellspacing`, `cellpadding`, and `valign` are obsolete. Just use CSS instead.

Not all presentational elements are obsolete. Some of them have been through a re-education program and given one more chance.

TURN & FACE THE STRANGE (CH-CH-CHANGES)

The `big` element is obsolete but the `small` element isn't. This apparent inconsistency has been resolved by redefining what `small` means. It no longer has the presentational connotation, "render this at a small size." Instead, it has the semantic value, "this is the small print," for legalese, or terms and conditions.

Of course, nine times out of ten you will want to render the small print at a small size, but the point is that the purely presentational meaning of the element has been superseded.

The `b` element used to mean, "render this in bold." Now it is used for some text "to be stylistically offset from the normal prose without conveying any extra importance." If the text has any extra importance, then the `strong` element would be more appropriate.

Similarly, the `i` element no longer means "italicize." It means the text is "in an alternate voice or mood." Again, the element doesn't imply any importance or emphasis. For emphasis, use the `em` element.

These changes might sound like word games. They are; but they also help to increase the device-independence of HTML5. If you think about the words "bold" and "italic," they only make sense for a visual medium such as a screen or a page. By removing the visual bias from the definitions of these elements, the specification remains relevant for non-visual user agents such as screen readers. It also encourages designers to think beyond visual rendering environments.

Out of cite

The `cite` element has been redefined in HTML5. Where it previously meant "a reference to other sources," it now means "the title of a work." Quite often, a cited reference will be the title of a work, such as a book or a film, but the source could just as easily be a person. Before HTML5, you could mark up that person's name using `cite`. Now that's expressly forbidden—so much for backwards compatibility.

The justification for this piece of revisionism goes something like this: browsers italicize the text between `<cite>` tags; titles of works are usually italicized; people's names aren't usually italicized; therefore the `cite` element shouldn't be used for marking up people's names.

That's just plain wrong. I'm in favor of HTML5 taking its lead from browsers, but this is a case of the tail wagging the dog.

Fortunately, no validator can possibly tell whether the text between opening and closing `<cite>` tags refers to a person or not, so there's nothing to stop us web designers from using the `cite` element in a sensible, backwards compatible way.

The a element on steroids

While the changes to previously existing elements involve creative wordplay, there's one element that's getting a supercharged makeover in HTML5.

The a element is, without a doubt, the most important element in HTML. It turns our text into hypertext. It is the connective tissue of the World Wide Web.

The a element has always been an inline element. If you wanted to make a headline and a paragraph into a hyperlink, you would have to use multiple a elements:

```
<h2><a href="/about">About me</a></h2>
<p><a href="/about">Find out what makes me tick.</a></p>
```

In HTML5, you can wrap multiple elements in a single a element:

```
<a href="/about">
  <h2>About me</h2>
  <p>Find out what makes me tick.</p>
</a>
```

The only caveat is that you can't nest an a element within another a element.

Wrapping multiple elements in a single a element might seem like a drastic change, but most browsers won't have to do much to support this new linking model. They already support it even though this kind of markup has never been technically legal until now.

This seems slightly counter-intuitive: Surely the browsers should be implementing an *existing* specification? Instead, the newest specification is documenting what browsers are already doing.

SHINY NEW TOYS: JAVASCRIPT APIs

If you're looking for documentation on CSS, you go to the CSS specifications. If you're looking for documentation on markup, you go to the HTML specifications. But where do you go for documentation on JavaScript APIs such as `document.write`, `innerHTML`, and `window.history`? The JavaScript specification is all about the programming language—you won't find any browser APIs there.

Until now, browsers have been independently creating and implementing JavaScript APIs, looking over one another's shoulders to see what the others are doing. HTML5 will document these APIs once and for all, which should ensure better compatibility.

It might sound strange to have JavaScript documentation in a markup specification, but remember that HTML5 started life as Web Apps 1.0. JavaScript is an indispensable part of making web applications.

Entire sections of the HTML5 specification are dedicated to new APIs for creating web applications. There's an `UndoManager` that allows the browser to keep track of changes to a document. There's a section on creating Offline Web Applications using a cache manifest. Drag and drop is described in detail.

As always, if there is an existing implementation, the specification will build upon it rather than reinvent the wheel. Microsoft's Internet Explorer has had a drag and drop API for years, so that's the basis for drag and drop in HTML5. Unfortunately, the Microsoft API is—to put it mildly—problematic. Maybe reinventing the wheel isn't such a bad idea if all you have to work with is a square wheel.

The APIs in HTML5 are very powerful. They are also completely over my head. I'll leave it to developers smarter than me to write about them. The APIs deserve their own separate book.

Meanwhile, there's still plenty of new stuff in HTML5 for us web designers to get excited about. This excitement commences in the very next chapter.

3 RICH MEDIA

THE HISTORY OF THE WEB is punctuated with technological improvements. One of the earliest additions to HTML was the `img` element, which fundamentally altered the web. Then, the introduction of JavaScript allowed the web to become a more dynamic environment. Later, the proliferation of Ajax made the web a viable option for full-fledged applications.

Web standards have advanced so much that it's now possible to build almost anything using HTML, CSS, and JavaScript—*almost* anything.

There are some gaps in the web standards palette. If you want to publish text and images, HTML and CSS are all you need. But if you want to publish audio or video, you'll need to use a plug-in technology such as Flash or Silverlight.

"Plug-in" is an accurate term for these technologies—they

help to fill the holes on the web. They make it relatively easy to get games, films, and music online. But these technologies are not open. They are not created by the community. They are under the control of individual companies.

Flash is a powerful technology, but using it sometimes feels like a devil's bargain. We gain the ability to publish rich media on the web, but in doing so, we lose some of our independence.

HTML5 is filling in the gaps. As such, it is in direct competition with proprietary technologies like Flash and Silverlight. But instead of requiring a plug-in, the rich media elements in HTML5 are native to the browser.

CANVAS

When the Mosaic browser added the ability to embed images within web pages, it gave the web a turbo boost. But images have remained static ever since. You can create animated gifs. You can use JavaScript to update an image's styles. You can generate an image dynamically on the server. But once an image has been served up to a browser, its contents cannot be updated.

The `canvas` element is an environment for creating dynamic images.

The element itself is very simple. All you specify within the opening tag are the dimensions:

```
<canvas id="my-first-canvas" width="360" height="240">
</canvas>
```

If you put anything between the opening and closing tags, only browsers that don't support canvas will see it (FIG 3.01):

```
<canvas id="my-first-canvas" width="360" height="240">
  <p>No canvas support? Have an old-fashioned image »
  instead:</p>
  <img src="puppy.jpg" alt="a cute puppy">
</canvas>
```

No canvas support?
Have an old-fashioned image instead:

FIG 3.01: Users without canvas support will see the image of a cute puppy.

All the hard work is done in JavaScript. First of all, you'll need to reference the canvas element and its context. The word "context" here simply means an API. For now, the only context is two-dimensional:

```
var canvas = document.getElementById('my-first-canvas');
var context = canvas.getContext('2d');
```

Now you can start drawing on the two-dimensional surface of the canvas element using the API documented in the HTML5 specification at http://bkaprt.com/html5/1.[1]

The 2D API offers a lot of the same tools that you find in a graphics program like Illustrator: strokes, fills, gradients, shadows, shapes, and Bézier curves. The difference is that, instead

1. The long URL: http://www.whatwg.org/specs/web-apps/current-work/multipage/the-canvas-element.html

of using a Graphical User Interface, you have to specify everything using JavaScript.

Dancing about architecture: drawing with code

This is how you specify that the stroke color should be red:

```
context.strokeStyle = '#990000';
```

Now anything you draw will have a red outline. For example, if you want to draw a rectangle, use this syntax:

```
strokeRect ( left, top, width, height )
```

If you want to draw a rectangle that's 100 by 50 pixels in size, positioned 20 pixels from the left and 30 pixels from the top of the `canvas` element, you'd write this (FIG 3.02):

```
context.strokeRect(20,30,100,50);
```

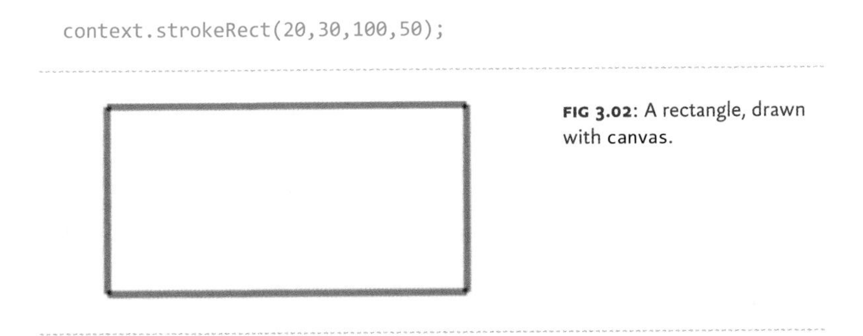

FIG 3.02: A rectangle, drawn with canvas.

That's one very simple example. The 2D API provides lots of methods: `fillStyle`, `fillRect`, `lineWidth`, `shadowColor` and many more.

In theory, any image that can be created in a program like Illustrator can be created in the `canvas` element. In practice, doing so would be laborious and could result in excessively long JavaScript. Besides, that isn't really the point of canvas.

Canvas. Huh! What is it good for?

It's all well and good using JavaScript and canvas to create images on the fly, but unless you're a hardcore masochist, what's the point?

The real power of canvas is that its contents can be updated at any moment, drawing new content based on the actions of the user. This ability to respond to user-triggered events makes it possible to create tools and games that would have previously required a plug-in technology such as Flash.

One of the first flagship demonstrations of the power of canvas came from Mozilla Labs. The Bespin application (https://bespin.mozilla.com) is a code editor that runs in the browser (FIG 3.03).

It is very powerful. It is very impressive. It is also a perfect example of what *not* to do with canvas.

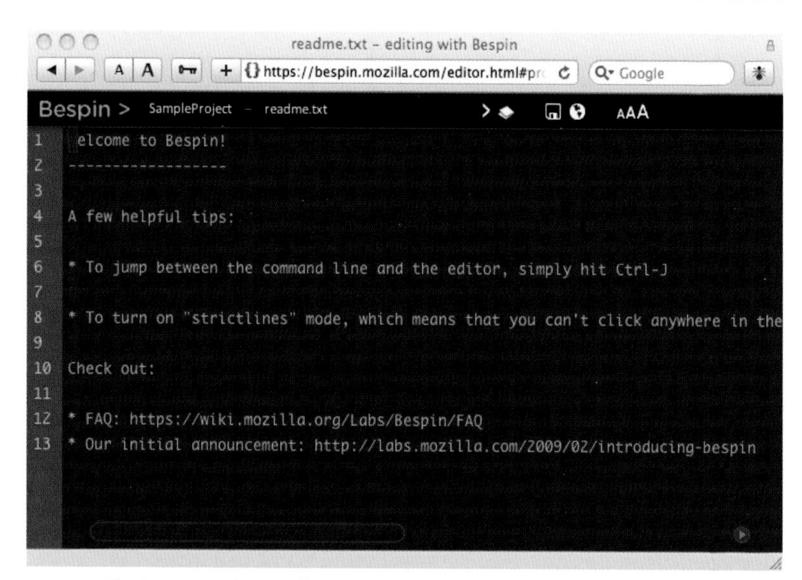

FIG 3.03: The Bespin application, built with canvas.

Access denied

A code editor, by its nature, handles text. The Bespin code editor handles text within the canvas element—except that it isn't really text anymore; it's a series of shapes that look like text.

Every document on the web can be described with a Document Object Model. This DOM can have many different nodes, the most important of which are element nodes, text nodes, and attributes. Those three building blocks are enough to put together just about any document you can imagine. The canvas element has no DOM. The content drawn within canvas cannot be represented as a tree of nodes.

Screen readers and other assistive technology rely on having access to a Document Object Model to make sense of a document. No DOM, no access.

The lack of accessibility in canvas is a big problem for HTML5. Fortunately there are some very smart people working together as a task force to come up with solutions (http://bkaprt.com/html5/2).[2]

Canvas accessibility is an important issue and I don't want any proposed solutions to be rushed. At the same time, I don't want canvas to hold up the rest of the HTML5 spec.

Clever canvas

Until the lack of accessibility is addressed, it might seem as though canvas is off-limits to web designers. But it ain't necessarily so.

Whenever I use JavaScript on a website, I use it as an enhancement. Visitors who don't have JavaScript still have access to all the content, but the experience might not be quite

2. The long URL: http://www.w3.org/WAI/PF/html-task-force

as dynamic as in a JavaScript-capable environment. This multi-tiered approach, called Unobtrusive JavaScript, can also be applied to canvas. Instead of using canvas to create content, use it to recycle existing content.

Suppose you have a table filled with data. You might want to illustrate the trends in the data using a graph. If the data is static, you can generate an image of a graph—using the Google Chart API, for example. If the data is editable, updating in response to user-triggered events, then canvas is a good tool for generating the changing graph. Crucially, the content represented within the `canvas` element is already accessible in the pre-existing `table` element.

The clever folks at Filament Group have put together a jQuery plug-in for that very situation (FIG 3.04; http://bkaprt.com/html5/3).[3]

There is another option. Canvas isn't the only API for generating dynamic images. SVG, Scalable Vector Graphics, is an

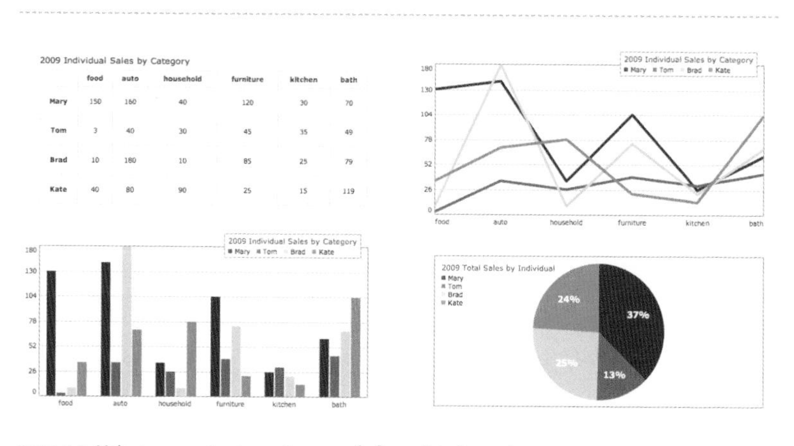
2009 Individual Sales by Category

	food	auto	household	furniture	kitchen	bath
Mary	150	160	40	120	30	70
Tom	3	40	30	45	35	49
Brad	10	180	10	85	25	79
Kate	40	80	90	25	15	119

FIG 3.04: Using canvas to generate a graph from data input by users.

3. The long URL: http://www.filamentgroup.com/lab/update_to_jquery_visualize_accessible_charts_with_html5_from_designing_with/

XML format that can describe the same kind of shapes as canvas. Because XML is a text-based data format, the contents of SVG are theoretically available to screen readers.

In practice, SVG hasn't captured the imagination of developers in the same way that canvas has. Even though canvas is the new kid on the block, it already enjoys excellent browser support. Safari, Firefox, Opera, and Chrome support canvas. There's even a JavaScript library that adds canvas support to Internet Explorer (http://bkaprt.com/html5/4).[4]

Given its mantras of "pave the cowpaths," and "don't reinvent the wheel," it might seem odd that the WHATWG would advocate canvas in HTML5 when SVG already exists. As is so often the case, the HTML5 specification is really just documenting what browsers already do. The canvas element wasn't dreamt up for HTML5; it was created by Apple and implemented in Safari. Other browser makers saw what Apple was doing, liked what they saw, and copied it.

It sounds somewhat haphazard, but this is often where our web standards come from. Microsoft, for example, created the `XMLHttpRequest` object for Internet Explorer 5 at the end of the 20th century. A decade later, every browser supports this feature and it's now a working draft in last call at the W3C.

In the Darwinian world of web browsers, canvas is spreading far and wide. If it can adapt for accessibility, its survival is ensured.

AUDIO

The first website I ever made was a showcase for my band. I wanted visitors to the site to be able to listen to the band's songs. That prompted my journey into the underworld to investigate the many formats and media players competing

4. The long URL: http://code.google.com/p/explorercanvas/

for my attention: QuickTime, Windows Media Player, Real Audio—I spent far too much time worrying about relative market share and cross-platform compatibility.

In the intervening years, the MP3 format has won the battle for ubiquity. But providing visitors with an easy way to listen to a sound file still requires a proprietary technology. The Flash player has won that battle.

Now HTML5 is stepping into the ring in an attempt to take on the reigning champion.

Embedding an audio file in an HTML5 document is simple:

```
<audio src="witchitalineman.mp3">
</audio>
```

That's a little too simple. You probably want to be a bit more specific about what the audio should do.

Suppose there's an evil bastard out there who hates the web and all who sail her. This person probably doesn't care that it's incredibly rude and stupid to embed an audio file that plays automatically. Thanks to the `autoplay` attribute, such malevolent ambitions can be realized:

```
<audio src="witchitalineman.mp3" autoplay>
</audio>
```

If you ever use the `autoplay` attribute in this way, I will hunt you down.

Notice that the `autoplay` attribute doesn't have a value. This is known as a Boolean attribute, named for that grand Cork mathematician George Boole.

Computer logic is based entirely on Boolean logic: an electric current is either flowing or it isn't; a binary value is either one or zero; the result of a computation is either true or false.

Don't confuse Boolean *attributes* with Boolean *values*. You'd be forgiven for thinking that a Boolean attribute would take the values "true" or "false." Actually, it's the very existence of the attribute that is Boolean in nature: either the attribute is included or it isn't. Even if you give the attribute a value, it will have no effect. Writing `autoplay="false"` or `autoplay="no thanks"` is the same as writing `autoplay`.

If you are using XHTML syntax, you can write `autoplay="autoplay"`. This is brought to you by the Department of Redundancy Department.

When an auto-playing audio file isn't evil enough, you can inflict even more misery by having the audio loop forever. Another Boolean attribute, called `loop`, fulfills this dastardly plan:

```
<audio src="witchitalineman.mp3" autoplay loop>
</audio>
```

Using the `loop` attribute in combination with the `autoplay` attribute in this way will renew my determination to hunt you down.

Out of control

The `audio` element can be used for good as well as evil. Giving users control over the playback of an audio file is a sensible idea that is easily accomplished using the Boolean attribute `controls`:

```
<audio src="witchitalineman.mp3" controls>
</audio>
```

The presence of the `controls` attribute prompts the browser to provide native controls for playing and pausing the audio, as well as adjusting the volume (FIG 3.05).

If you're not happy with the browser's native controls, you can create your own. Using JavaScript, you can interact with

FIG 3.05: Use `controls` to display play, pause, and volume controls for your audio.

the `Audio` API, which gives you access to methods such as `play` and `pause` and properties such as `volume`. Here's a quick 'n' dirty example using `button` elements and nasty inline event handlers (FIG 3.06):

```
<audio id="player" src="witchitalineman.mp3">
</audio>
<div>
  <button »
  onclick="document.getElementById('player').play()"> »
  Play
  </button>
  <button »
  onclick="document.getElementById('player').pause()"> »
  Pause
  </button>
  <button »
  onclick="document.getElementById('player').volume »
  += 0.1">
  Volume Up
  </button>
  <button »
  onclick="document.getElementById('player').volume »
  -= 0.1">
  Volume Down
  </button>
</div>
```

Buffering

At one point, the HTML5 spec included another Boolean attribute for the `audio` element. The `autobuffer` attribute was more polite and thoughtful than the nasty `autoplay` attribute. It provided a way for authors to inform the browser

Play | Pause | Volume Up | Volume Down

FIG 3.06: The controls produced by the button elements.

that—although the audio file shouldn't play automatically—it will probably be played at some point, so the browser should start pre-loading the file in the background.

This would have been a useful attribute, but unfortunately Safari went a step further. It preloaded audio files regardless of whether or not the `autobuffer` attribute was present. Remember that because `autobuffer` was a Boolean attribute, there was no way to tell Safari not to preload the audio: `autobuffer="false"` was the same as `autobuffer="true"` or any other value (http://bkaprt.com/html5/5).[5]

The `autobuffer` attribute has now been replaced with the `preload` attribute. This isn't a Boolean attribute. It can take three possible values: `none`, `auto`, and `metadata`. Using `preload="none"`, you can now explicitly tell browsers not to pre-load the audio:

```
<audio src="witchitalineman.mp3" controls preload="none">
</audio>
```

If you only have one audio element on a page, you might want to use `preload="auto"`, but the more `audio` elements you have, the more your visitors' bandwidth is going to get hammered by excessive preloading.

You play to-may-to, I play to-mah-to

The `audio` element appears to be nigh-on perfect. Surely there must be a catch somewhere? There is.

The problem with the `audio` element isn't in the specification. The problem lies with audio formats.

5. The long URL: https://bugs.webkit.org/show_bug.cgi?id=25267

Although the MP3 format has become ubiquitous, it is not an open format. Because the format is patent-encumbered, technologies can't decode MP3 files without paying the patent piper. That's fine for corporations like Apple or Adobe, but it's not so easy for smaller companies or open-source groups. Hence, Safari will happily play back MP3 files while Firefox will not.

There are other audio formats out there. The Vorbis codec—usually delivered as an `.ogg` file—isn't crippled by any patents. Firefox supports Ogg Vorbis—but Safari doesn't.

Fortunately, there's a way to use the `audio` element without having to make a Sophie's Choice between file formats. Instead of using the `src` attribute in the opening `<audio>` tag, you can specify multiple file formats using the `source` element:

```
<audio controls>
  <source src="witchitalineman.ogg">
  <source src="witchitalineman.mp3">
</audio>
```

A browser that can play back Ogg Vorbis files will look no further than the first `source` element. A browser that can play MP3 files but not Ogg Vorbis files will skip over the first `source` element and play the file in the second `source` element.

You can help the browsers by providing the mime types for each source file:

```
<audio controls>
  <source src="witchitalineman.ogg" type="audio/ogg">
  <source src="witchitalineman.mp3" type="audio/mpeg">
</audio>
```

The source element is a standalone—or "void"—element, so if you are using XHTML syntax, remember to include a trailing slash at the end of each <source /> tag.

Falling back

The ability to specify multiple source elements is very useful. But there are some browsers that don't support the audio element at all yet. Can you guess which browser I might be talking about?

Internet Explorer and its ilk need to be spoon-fed audio files the old-fashioned way, via Flash. The content model of the audio element supports this. Anything between the opening and closing <audio> tags that isn't a source element will be exposed to browsers that don't understand the audio element:

```
<audio controls>
  <source src="witchitalineman.ogg" type="audio/ogg">
  <source src="witchitalineman.mp3" type="audio/mpeg">
  <object type="application/x-shockwave-flash" »
  data="player.swf?soundFile=witchitalineman.mp3">
    <param name="movie" »
    value="player.swf?soundFile=witchitalineman.mp3">
  </object>
</audio>
```

The object element in this example will only be exposed to browsers that don't support the audio element.

You can go even further. The object element also allows you to include fallback content. That means you can provide a good old-fashioned hyperlink as a last resort:

```
<audio controls>
  <source src="witchitalineman.ogg" type="audio/ogg">
  <source src="witchitalineman.mp3" type="audio/mpeg">
```

```
    <object type="application/x-shockwave-flash" »
    data="player.swf?soundFile=witchitalineman.mp3">
      <param name="movie" »
      value="player.swf?soundFile=witchitalineman.mp3">
      <a href="witchitalineman.mp3">Download the song</a>
    </object>
  </audio>
```

This example has four levels of graceful degradation:

- The browser supports the audio element and the Ogg Vorbis format.
- The browser supports the audio element and the MP3 format.
- The browser doesn't support the audio element but does have the Flash plug-in installed.
- The browser doesn't support the audio element and doesn't have the Flash plug-in installed.

Access all areas

The content model of the audio element is very useful for providing fallback content. Fallback content is not the same as accessibility content.

Suppose there's a transcript to go along with an audio file. This is *not* the way to mark it up:

```
<audio controls>
  <source src="witchitalineman.ogg" type="audio/ogg">
  <source src="witchitalineman.mp3" type="audio/mpeg">
  <p>I am a lineman for the county...</p>
</audio>
```

The transcript will only be visible to browsers that don't support the audio element. Marking up the non-audio content in that way isn't going to help a deaf user with a good browser. Besides, so-called accessibility content is often very useful for everyone, so why hide it?

```
<audio controls>
  <source src="witchitalineman.ogg" type="audio/ogg">
  <source src="witchitalineman.mp3" type="audio/mpeg">
</audio>
<p>I am a lineman for the county...</p>
```

VIDEO

If browser-native audio is exciting, the prospect of browser-native video has web designers salivating in anticipation. As bandwidth has increased, video content has grown increasingly popular. The Flash plug-in is currently the technology of choice for displaying video on the web. HTML5 could change that.

The `video` element works just like the `audio` element. It has the optional `autoplay`, `loop`, and `preload` attributes. You can specify the location of the video file by either using the `src` attribute on the `video` element or by using `source` elements nested within the opening and closing `<video>` tags. You can let the browser take care of providing a user interface with the `controls` attribute or you can script your own controls.

The main difference between audio and video content is that movies, by their nature, will take up more room on the screen, so you'll probably want to provide dimensions:

```
<video src="movie.mp4" controls width="360" height="240">
</video>
```

You can choose a representative image for the video and tell the browser to display it using the `poster` attribute (FIG 3.07):

```
<video src="movie.mp4" controls width="360" »
height="240" poster="placeholder.jpg">
</video>
```

FIG 3.07: This placeholder image is displayed using the `poster` attribute.

The battleground of competing video formats is even bloodier than that of audio. Some of the big players are MP4—which is patent-encumbered—and Theora Video, which isn't. Once again, you'll need to provide alternate encodings and fallback content:

```
<video controls width="360" height="240" »
poster="placeholder.jpg">
  <source src="movie.ogv" type="video/ogg">
  <source src="movie.mp4" type="video/mp4">
  <object type="application/x-shockwave-flash" »
  width="360" height="240" »
  data="player.swf?file=movie.mp4">
    <param name="movie" »
    value="player.swf?file=movie.mp4">
    <a href="movie.mp4">Download the movie</a>
  </object>
</video>
```

The authors of the HTML5 specification had originally hoped to specify a baseline level of format support. Alas, the browser makers could not agree on a single format.

Going native

The ability to embed video natively in web pages could be the most exciting addition to HTML since the introduction of the `img` element. Big players like Google have not been shy in expressing their enthusiasm. You can get a taste for what they have planned for YouTube at http://youtube.com/HTML5.

One of the problems with relying on a plug-in for rich media is that plug-in content is sandboxed from the rest of the document. Having native rich media elements in HTML means that they play nicely with the other browser technologies—JavaScript and CSS.

The `video` element is not only scriptable, it is also styleable (FIG 3.08).

FIG 3.08: The video element, styled.

Try doing *that* to a plug-in.

Audio and video are welcome additions to HTML5, but the web isn't a broadcast medium—it's interactive. Forms are the oldest and most powerful way of enabling interaction. In Chapter 4, we'll take a look at how forms are getting an upgrade in HTML5.

4 WEB FORMS 2.0

WHEN JAVASCRIPT WAS INTRODUCED into web browsers, it was immediately seized upon for two tasks: Image rollovers and form enhancements. When CSS came along with its `:hover` pseudo-class, web designers no longer needed to reach for JavaScript just to achieve a simple rollover effect.

This is a recurring trend. If a pattern is popular enough, it will almost certainly evolve from requiring a scripted solution to something more declarative. That's why CSS3 introduces even more animation capabilities that previously required JavaScript.

When it comes to enhancing forms, CSS has its limitations. That's where HTML5 comes in. Following the same migratory pattern from scripted to declarative solutions, the specification introduces many new form enhancements.

These features were originally part of a WHATWG specification called Web Forms 2.0, based upon existing work at the W3C. That specification has now been rolled into HTML5.

PLACEHOLDER

Here's a common DOM Scripting pattern, often used for search forms:

1. When a form field has no value, insert some placeholder text into it.
2. When the user focuses on that field, remove the placeholder text.
3. If the user leaves the field and the field still has no value, reinstate the placeholder text.

The placeholder text is usually displayed in a lighter shade than an actual form field value—either through CSS, JavaScript, or a combination of both.

In an HTML5 document, you can simply use the `placeholder` attribute (FIG 4.01):

```
<label for="hobbies">Your hobbies</label>
<input id="hobbies" name="hobbies" type="text" »
placeholder="Owl stretching">
```

The `placeholder` attribute works wonderfully in the browsers that support it, but, alas, that's a fairly small subset of browsers right now. It's up to you to decide how you want to deal with other, non-supporting browsers.

You might decide not to do anything at all. After all, the functionality is "nice to have," not "must have." Alternatively, you

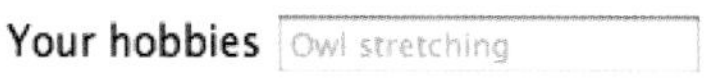

Your hobbies Owl stretching

FIG 4.01: "Owl stretching" appears in the input field via the `placeholder` attribute.

might decide to fall back on a JavaScript solution. In that case, you need to make sure that the JavaScript solution is only applied to browsers that don't understand the `placeholder` attribute.

Here's a generic little JavaScript function that tests whether an element supports a particular attribute:

```
function elementSupportsAttribute(element,attribute) {
  var test = document.createElement(element);
  if (attribute in test) {
    return true;
  } else {
    return false;
  }
}
```

This works by creating a "phantom" element in memory—but not in your document—and then checking to see if the prototype for that element has a property with the same name as the attribute you are testing for. The function will return either `true` or `false`.

Using this function, you can make sure that a JavaScript solution is only provided to browsers that don't support `placeholder`:

```
if (!elementSupportsAttribute('input','placeholder')) {
  // JavaScript fallback goes here.
}
```

AUTOFOCUS

"Hi. I'm the auto-focus pattern. You may remember me from such websites as 'Google: I'm Feeling Lucky' and 'Twitter: What's happening?'"

This is a simple one-step pattern, easily programmed in JavaScript:

1. When the document loads, automatically focus one particular form field.

HTML5 allows you to do this using the Boolean `autofocus` attribute:

```
<label for="status">What's happening?</label>
<input id="status" name="status" type="text" autofocus>
```

The only problem with this pattern is that it can be annoying as hell. When I'm surfing the web, I often hit the space bar to scroll down to content "below the fold." On sites like Twitter that use the auto-focus pattern, I find myself filling up a form field with spaces instead.

I can see why the `autofocus` attribute has been added to HTML5—it's paving a cowpath—but I worry about the usability of this pattern, be it scripted or native. This feature could be helpful, but it could just as easily be infuriating. Please think long and hard before implementing this pattern.

One of the advantages in moving this pattern from scripting to markup is that, in theory, browsers can offer users a preference option to disable auto-focusing. In practice, no browser does this yet, but the pattern is still quite young. Currently, the only way to disable scripted auto-focusing is to disable JavaScript completely. It works, but it's a heavy-handed solution, like gouging out your eyes to avoid bright lights.

As with the `placeholder` attribute, you can test for `autofocus` support and fall back to a scripted solution:

```
if (!elementSupportsAttribute('input','autofocus')){
  document.getElementById('status').focus();
}
```

The `autofocus` attribute doesn't only work on the `input` element; it can be used on any kind of form field, such as `textarea` or `select`, but it can only be used once per document.

REQUIRED

One of the most common uses of JavaScript is client-side form validation. Once again, HTML5 is moving this solution from scripting to markup. Just add the Boolean attribute `required`:

```
<label for="pass">Your password</label>
<input id="pass" name="pass" type="password" required>
```

Theoretically, this allows browsers to prevent form submissions if required fields haven't been filled out. Even though browsers aren't doing that yet, you can still make use of the `required` attribute in your JavaScript form validation. Instead of keeping a list of all the required fields in your script or adding `class="required"` to your markup, you can now check for the existence of the `required` attribute.

AUTOCOMPLETE

Browsers don't simply display web pages. Most browsers have additional features designed to enhance usability, security, or convenience when surfing the web's tide. Automatically filling in forms is one such feature. Most of the time, it's very useful, but occasionally it can be annoying or even downright dangerous. I don't mind if my browser remembers my contact details, but I probably don't want it to remember the log-in for my bank account, just in case my computer is stolen.

HTML5 allows you to disable auto-completion on a per-form or per-field basis. The `autocomplete` attribute isn't Boolean, yet it can only take two possible values: "on" or "off":

```
<form action="/selfdestruct" autocomplete="off">
```

By default, browsers will assume an autocomplete value of "on," allowing them to pre-fill the form.

You can have your auto-completion cake and eat it. If you want to allow pre-filling for a form but disable pre-filling for just one or two fields in that form, you can do so:

```
<input type="text" name="onetimetoken" »
autocomplete="off">
```

There isn't any JavaScript fallback for browsers that don't support the autocomplete attribute. In this case, the new HTML5 attribute is augmenting an existing browser behavior rather than replacing a scripted solution.

The ability to disable auto-completion in browsers might seem like a strange addition to the HTML5 specification. HTML5 is supposed to be codifying prevalent patterns and this isn't a very common use case. But given the potential security risks that auto-completion enables, it makes sense to allow website owners to override this particular browser feature.

DATALIST

The new datalist element allows you to crossbreed a regular input element with a select element. Using the list attribute, you can associate a list of options with an input field (FIG 4.02):

```
<label for="homeworld">Your home planet</label>
<input type="text" name="homeworld" id="homeworld" »
list="planets">
<datalist id="planets">
  <option value="Mercury">
  <option value="Venus">
```

```
    <option value="Earth">
    <option value="Mars">
    <option value="Jupiter">
    <option value="Saturn">
    <option value="Uranus">
    <option value="Neptune">
  </datalist>
```

This allows users to select an option from the list provided or to type in a value that isn't in the list at all. This is very handy for situations that would normally require an extra form field labeled, "If 'other', please specify . . ." (FIG 4.03).

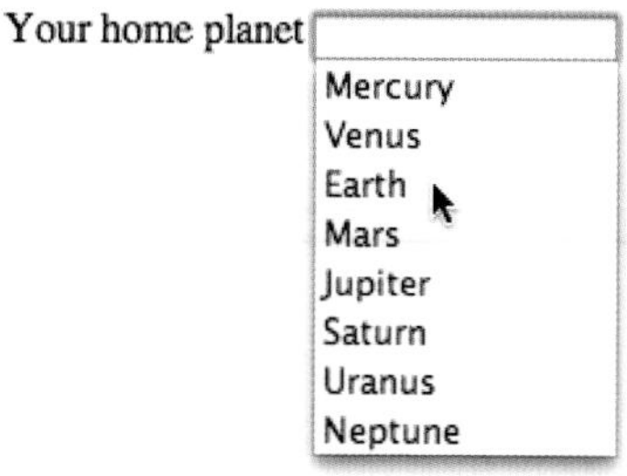

FIG 4.02: The new datalist element.

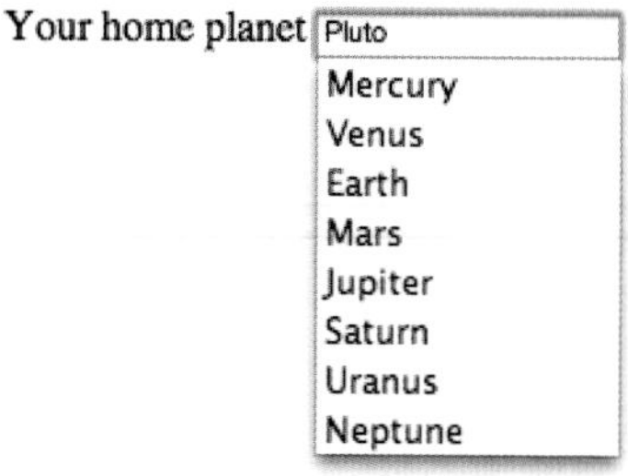

FIG 4.03: The datalist element, showing that the user can type in a value that is not in the list.

The datalist element is a nice, unobtrusive enhancement to a form field. If a browser doesn't support datalist, then the form field behaves as a normal input.

INPUT TYPES

The type attribute of the input element is being greatly expanded in HTML5. There are so many cowpaths to pave, it's like doing construction work in the aftermath of a stampede.

Searching

An `input` element with a `type` value of "search" will behave much the same way as an input element with a `type` value of "text":

```
<label for="query">Search</label>
<input id="query" name="query" type="search">
```

The only difference between "text" and "search" is that a browser might display a search input differently to be more consistent with the styling of search fields in the operating system. That's exactly what Safari does (FIG 4.04).

FIG 4.04: Safari styles search inputs to be consistent with Mac OS

Contact details

There are three new `type` values for specific kinds of contact details: email addresses, websites, and telephone numbers:

```
<label for="email">Email address</label>
<input id="email" name="email" type="email">
<label for="website">Website</label>
<input id="website" name="website" type="url">
<label for="phone">Telephone</label>
<input id="phone" name="phone" type="tel">
```

Once again, these fields will behave in the same way as text inputs, but browsers now have a bit more information about the kind of data expected in the field.

Safari claims to support these new input types but a quick look at a form in the desktop browser reveals no differences to simply using `type="text"`. However, if you start interacting with the same form in Mobile Safari, the differences become apparent. The browser displays a different on-screen keyboard depending on the value of the `type` attribute (FIG 4.05).

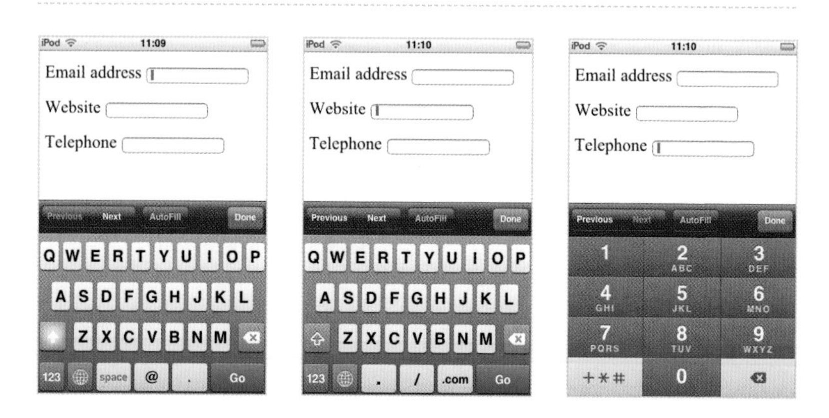

FIG 4.05: Mobile Safari shows a different on-screen keyboard depending on the value of the type attribute.

Subtly played, Webkit, subtly played.

Sliders

Many JavaScript libraries offer pre-built widgets that you can use in your web applications. They work fine—as long as JavaScript is enabled. It would be nice if our users didn't have to download a JavaScript file every time we want to add an interesting control to our pages.

A classic example is a slider control. Until now, we've had to use JavaScript to emulate this kind of interactive element. In

HTML5, thanks to `type="range"`, browsers can now offer a native control:

```
<label for="amount">How much?</label>
<input id="amount" name="amount" type="range">
```

Both Safari and Opera currently support this input type, offering similar-looking controls (FIG 4.06).

How much?

FIG 4.06: The range input type in both Safari and Opera.

By default, the input will accept a range from zero to one hundred. You can set your own minimum and maximum values using the `min` and `max` attributes:

```
<label for="rating">Your rating</label>
<input id="rating" name="rating" type="range" »
min="1" max="5">
```

That's all well and good for Safari and Opera users; other browsers will simply display a regular text input. That's probably fine, but you might want to use a JavaScript fallback for browsers that don't support `type="range"`.

Testing

Testing for native support of input types requires a similar trick to the test for attribute support. Once again, you will need to create a "phantom" `input` element in memory. Then, set the `type` attribute to the value you want to test. When you query the value of the `type` property, if you get back a value of "text," then you'll know that the browser doesn't support the value that you set.

Here's some sample code, although I'm sure you can write something far more elegant than this:

```
function inputSupportsType(test) {
  var input = document.createElement('input');
  input.setAttribute('type',test);
  if (input.type == 'text') {
    return false;
  } else {
    return true;
  }
}
```

You can then use this function to ensure that a JavaScript widget is only provided to browsers that don't natively support a particular input type:

```
if (!inputSupportsType('range')) {
  // JavaScript fallback goes here.
}
```

A native input control will certainly load faster than a scripted solution that needs to wait until the DOM has finished loading. A native control will also usually be more accessible than a scripted control, although—bizarrely—Safari's `range` control currently isn't keyboard-accessible!

Spinners

A browser-native `range` control doesn't expose the underlying value to the user. Instead, the number is translated into the graphical representation of a slider widget. That's fine for certain kinds of data. Other kinds of data work best when the user can see and choose the numerical value. That's where `type="number"` comes in:

```
<label for="amount">How much?</label>
<input id="amount" name="amount" type="number" »
min="5" max="20">
```

As well as allowing the user to input a value directly into a text field, browsers can also display "spinner" controls to allow users to increase or decrease the value (FIG 4.07).

How much?

FIG 4.07: Spinner controls where `type="number"` is used.

The `number` input type is a hybrid of `text` and `range`. It allows users to enter values directly, like a `text` field, but it also allows browsers to ensure that only numerical values are entered, like a `range` control.

Dates and times

One of the most popular JavaScript widgets is the calendar picker. You know the drill: you're booking a flight or creating an event and you need to choose a date. Up pops a little calendar for you to choose a date from.

These calendar widgets all do the same thing, but you'll find that they're implemented slightly differently on each site. A native calendar widget would smooth away the inconsistencies and reduce cognitive load during the date-picking process.

HTML5 introduces a raft of input types specifically for dates and times:

- `date` is for a year, month, and day.
- `datetime` is for a year, month, and day in combination with hours, minutes, and seconds and time zone information.
- `datetime-local` is the same but without the time zone information.
- `time` is for hours, minutes, and seconds.
- `month` is for a year and a month but without a day.

All of these input types will record timestamps with some subset of the standardized format YYYY-MM-DDThh:mm:ss.Z (Y is year, M is month, D is day, h is hour, m is minute, s is second, and Z is timezone). Take, for example, the date and time at which World War One ended, 11:11am on November 11th, 1918:

- date: 1918-11-11
- datetime: 1918-11-11T11:11:00+01
- datetime-local: 1918-11-11T11:11:00
- time: 11:11:00
- month: 1918-11

There is no year input type, although there is a week input type that takes a number between 1 and 53 in combination with a year.

Using the date and time input types is straightforward:

```
<label for="dtstart">Start date</label>
<input id="dtstart" name="dtstart" type="date">
```

Opera implements these input types using its patented ugly-stick technology (FIG 4.08).

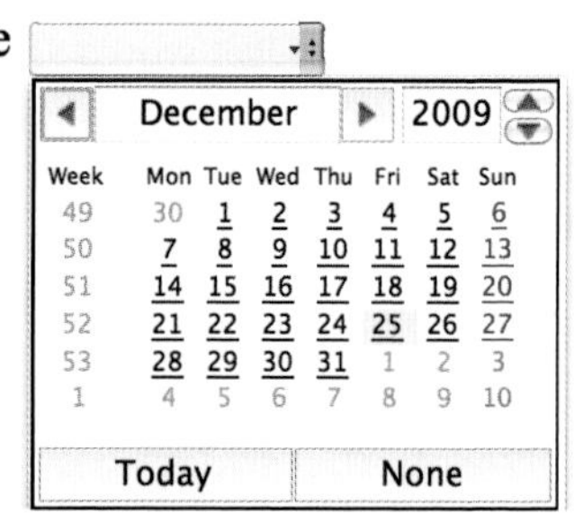

FIG 4.08: Opera's native calendar display, with the ugly-stick.

As always, browsers that don't support these input types will fall back to displaying a regular text input. In that situation, you could ask your users to enter dates and times in the ISO format or you could use your JavaScript library of choice to generate a widget. Make sure to check for native support first:

```
if (!inputSupportsType('date')) {
  // Generate a calendar widget here.
}
```

Even the most elegantly written JavaScript calendar widget is going to require some complex code to generate the table of days and handle the date-picking events. Browser-native calendar widgets should be considerably smoother and faster, as well as being consistent from site to site.

Color pickers

Perhaps the most ambitious widget replacement in HTML5 is the `color` input type. This accepts values in the familiar Hexadecimal format: `#000000` for black, `#FFFFFF` for white.

```
<label for="bgcolor">Background color</label>
<input id="bgcolor" name="bgcolor" type="color">
```

The plan is for browsers to implement native color pickers like the ones in just about every other application on your computer. So far, no browsers have done this but when they do, it will be, like, totally awesome.

In the meantime, you can use a JavaScript solution, but be sure to test for native support, so your code is future-proofed for tomorrow's browsers.

Rolling your own

All of these new input types serve two purposes: they allow browsers to display native controls suited to the expected input data, and to validate the value entered. These additions to HTML5 cover the majority of scenarios, but you still might find that you need to validate a value that doesn't fall under any of the new categories.

The good news is that you can use the `pattern` attribute to specify exactly what kind of value is expected. The bad news is that you have to use a regular expression:

```
<label for="zip">US Zip code</label>
<input id="zip" name="zip" pattern="[\d]{5}(-[\d]{4})">
```

Most of the time, you'll never need to use the `pattern` attribute. On the occasions that you do, you have my sympathy.

LOOKING TO THE FUTURE

Forms have been given a huge boost in HTML5. Much of the burden that has traditionally been carried by JavaScript is shifting onto the shoulders of markup. Right now, we're in a transitional phase where some of that functionality is supported by some browsers. We can't ditch our JavaScript just yet, but we're not too far away from a brighter future.

Client-side validation is going to get a whole lot easier—although you shouldn't ever rely on it; always validate form values on the server as well. Generating form controls will no longer require that your users download a JavaScript library; it will all be handled natively in the browser.

I'm sure you can see the benefits to having native browser controls for calendars and sliders, but I bet you're wondering: "Can I style them?"

It's a good question. For the time being, the answer is "no." Take it up with the CSS Working Group.

This might be a deal breaker for you. If you feel that a particular browser's implementation of a form element is less than finessed, you might prefer to use a JavaScript widget that gives you more control.

I'd like you to think about a different question: "*Should* I style them?"

Remember, the web isn't about control. If a visitor to your site is familiar with using a browser's native form doodad, you won't be doing them any favors if you override the browser functionality with your own widget, even if you think your widget looks better.

Personally, I'd like to see browser vendors competing on the prettiness and usability of their HTML5 form controls. That's a browser war I could support.

Let's put forms to one side now, and take a look at the juicy new semantics in HTML5.

5 SEMANTICS

HTML DOESN'T PROVIDE A HUGE NUMBER OF ELEMENTS for us to work with. The selection available is more like that of a corner store than a Walmart.

We have paragraphs, lists, and headlines but we don't have events, news stories, or recipes. HTML gives us an element for marking up a string as an abbreviation, but it doesn't give us an element for marking up a number as a price.

Clearly, this limitation hasn't been a show-stopper; just look at the amazing variety of websites out there. Even though HTML might not provide a specific element for marking up a particular piece of content, it provides just enough flexibility to be "good enough."

To paraphrase Winston Churchill, HTML is the worst form of markup except all the others that have been tried.

EXTENSIBILITY

Other markup languages allow you to invent any element you want. In XML, if you want an `event` element or a `price` element, you just go right ahead and create it. The downside to this freedom is that you then have to teach a parser what `event` or `price` means. The advantage to HTML's limited set of elements is that every user agent knows about every element. Browsers have a built-in knowledge of HTML. That wouldn't be possible if we were allowed to make up element names.

HTML provides a handy escape clause that allows web designers to add more semantic value to elements: the `class` attribute. This attribute allows us to label specific instances of an element as being a special class or type of that element. The fact that browsers don't understand the vocabulary we use in our `class` attributes doesn't affect the rendering of our documents.

If, at this point, you're thinking "Wait a minute; aren't classes for CSS?" then you're half right. The CSS class selector is one example of a technology that makes use of the `class` attribute but it isn't the *only* reason for using classes. Classes can also be used in DOM Scripting. They can even be used by browsers if the class names follow an agreed convention, as is the case with microformats.

Microformats

Microformats are a set of conventions which are agreed upon by a community. These formats use the `class` attribute to plug some of the more glaring holes in HTML: hCard for contact details, hCalendar for events, hAtom for news stories. Because there is a community consensus on what class names to use, there are now parsers and browser extensions that work with those specific patterns.

Microformats are limited by design. They don't attempt to solve every possible use case. Instead, they aim for the "low-hanging fruit." They solve 80% of the use cases with 20% of the effort. Deciding what qualifies as "low-hanging fruit" is pretty straightforward: Just look at what kind of content people are already marking up. In other words, pave the cowpaths.

Sound familiar? Microformats and HTML5 are built on very similar philosophies. In fact, the way I described microformats—conventions agreed upon by a community—could just as easily be applied to HTML5.

Boiling the ocean

The way that the microformats process has been used as a template for developing HTML5 isn't to everyone's taste. While the 80/20 rule is good enough for the rough 'n' ready world of class names, is it really good enough for the most important markup language in the world?

Some people feel that HTML needs to be infinitely extensible. That means it isn't enough to provide solutions to the majority of use cases; the language must provide a solution to any possible use case.

Perhaps the most eloquent argument for this kind of extensibility came from John Allsopp in his superb *A List Apart* article, "Semantics in HTML5" (http://bkaprt.com/html5/6):[1]

> *We don't need to add specific terms to the vocabulary of HTML, we need to add a mechanism that allows semantic richness to be added to a document as required.*

Technologies already exist to do just that. RDFa allows authors to embed custom vocabularies within HTML

1. The long URL: http://www.alistapart.com/articles/semanticsinHTML5

documents. But unlike microformats—which simply use an agreed set of class names—RDFa uses namespaces to allow an infinite variety of formats. So where a microformat might use markup such as `<h1 class="summary">`, RDFa would use `<h1 property="myformat:summary">`.

There's no doubt that RDFa is potentially very powerful, but its expressiveness comes at a price. Namespaces introduce an extra layer of complexity that doesn't sit well with the relatively simple nature of HTML.

The namespace debate isn't new. In a blog post from a few years back, Mark Nottingham mused on the potentially destructive side-effects (http://bkaprt.com/html5/7):[2]

> *What I found interesting about HTML extensibility was that namespaces weren't necessary; Netscape added blink, MSFT added marquee, and so forth. I'd put forth that having namespaces in HTML from the start would have had the effect of legitimising and institutionalising the differences between different browsers instead of (eventually) converging on the same solution.*

Rather than infinite extensibility, that's a powerful argument for a limited vocabulary based on community consensus.

HTML5 will probably ship with some kind of method for extending its native semantics. The `class` attribute is still in there of course, so microformats will continue to work as they always have. HTML5 might be altered to become compatible with RDFa, or it might use its own "microdata" vocabulary. In either case, such extensibility will probably be of very little interest to most web designers. What really matters are the native semantics, agreed upon by a community and implemented by browser vendors.

2. The long URL: http://www.mnot.net/blog/2006/04/07/extensibility

NEW ELEMENTS

HTML5 introduces a handful of new inline elements to augment our existing arsenal of `span`, `strong`, `em`, `abbr`, et al. Oh, and we don't call them "inline" anymore. Instead, they describe "text-level semantics."

mark

When browsing a list of search results, you'll often see the search term highlighted within each result. You could mark up each instance of the search term with a `span` element, but `span` is a semantically meaningless crutch, good for little more than hanging classes off for styling.

You could use `em` or `strong` but that wouldn't be semantically accurate; you don't want to place any importance on the search term, you simply want it to be highlighted somehow.

Enter the `mark` element:

```
<h1>Search results for 'unicorn'</h1>
<ol>
  <li><a href="http://clearleft.com/">
  Riding the UX <mark>unicorn</mark> across »
  the rainbow of the web.
  </a></li>
</ol>
```

The `mark` element doesn't attach any importance to the content within it, other than to show that it's currently of interest. As the specification says, `mark` denotes "a run of text in one document marked or highlighted for reference purposes, due to its relevance in another context."

The `mark` element is permitted in contexts other than search results, but I'm damned if I can think of a single such example.

time

hCalendar is one of the most popular microformats because it scratches a very common itch: marking up events so that users can add them straight to their calendar.

The only tricky bit in hCalendar is describing dates and times in a machine-readable way. Humans like to describe dates as "May 25th" or "next Wednesday" but parsers expect a nicely-formated ISO date: YYYY-MM-DDThh:mm:ss.

The microformats community came up with some clever solutions to this problem, such as using the `abbr` element:

```
<abbr class="dtstart" title="1992-01-12">
  January 12th, 1992
</abbr>
```

If using the `abbr` element in this way makes you feel a little queasy, there are plenty of other ways of marking up machine-readable dates and times in microformats using the class-value pattern. In HTML5, the issue is solved with the new `time` element:

```
<time class="dtstart" datetime="1992-01-12">
  January 12th, 1992
</time>
```

The `time` element can be used for dates, times, or combinations of both:

```
<time datetime="17:00">5pm</time>
<time datetime="2010-04-07">April 7th</time>
<time datetime="2010-04-07T17:00">5pm on April 7th</time>
```

You don't have to put the datetime value inside the `datetime` attribute—but if you don't, then you must expose the value to the end user:

```
<time>2010-04-07</time>
```

meter

The meter element can be used to mark up measurements, provided that those measurements are part of a scale with minimum and maximum values.

```
<meter>9 out of 10 cats</meter>
```

You don't have to expose the maximum value if you don't want to. You can use the max attribute instead:

```
<meter max="10">9 cats</meter>
```

There's a corresponding min attribute. You also get high, low, and optimum attributes to play with. If you want, you can even hide the measurement itself inside a value attribute.

```
<meter low="-273" high="100" min="12" max="30" »
optimum="21" value="25">
  It's quite warm for this time of year.
</meter>
```

progress

While meter is good for describing something that has already been measured, the progress element allows you to mark up a value that is in the process of changing:

```
Your profile is <progress>60%</progress> complete.
```

Once again, you have min, max, and value attributes if you want to use them:

```
<progress min="0" max="100" value="60"></progress>
```

The progress element is most useful when used in combination with DOM Scripting. You can use JavaScript to dynamically update the value, allowing the browser to communicate that change to the user—very handy for Ajax file uploads.

STRUCTURE

Back in 2005, Google did some research to find out what kind of low-hanging fruit could be found on the cowpaths of the web (http://code.google.com/webstats/).

A parser looked at over a billion web pages and tabulated the most common class names. The results were unsurprising. Class names such as "header," "footer," and "nav" were prevalent. These emergent semantics map nicely to some of the new structural elements introduced in HTML5.

section

The section element is used for grouping together thematically-related content. That sounds a lot like the div element, which is often used as a generic content container. The difference is that div has no semantic meaning; it doesn't tell you anything about the content within. The section element, on the other hand, is used explicitly for grouping related content.

You might be able to replace some of your div elements with section elements, but remember to always ask yourself, "Is all of the content related?"

```
<section>
  <h1>DOM Scripting</h1>
  <p>The book is aimed at designers »
  rather than programmers.</p>
  <p>By Jeremy Keith</p>
</section>
```

header

The HTML5 spec describes the `header` element as a container for "a group of introductory or navigational aids." That sounds reasonable. That's the kind of content I would expect to find in a masthead, and the word "header" is often used as a synonym for masthead.

There's a crucial difference between the `header` element in HTML5 and the generally accepted use of the word "header" or "masthead." There's usually only one masthead in a page, but a document can have multiple `header` elements. You can use the `header` element within a `section` element, for example. In fact, you probably *should* use a `header` within a `section`. The specification describes the `section` element as "a thematic grouping of content, *typically with a heading*."

```
<section>
  <header>
    <h1>DOM Scripting</h1>
  </header>
  <p>The book is aimed at designers »
  rather than programmers.</p>
  <p>By Jeremy Keith</p>
</section>
```

A `header` will usually appear at the top of a document or section, but it doesn't have to. It is defined by its content—introductory or navigational aids—rather than its position.

footer

Like the `header` element, `footer` sounds like it's a description of position but, as with `header`, this isn't the case. Instead, the `footer` element should contain information about its containing element: who wrote it, copyright information, links to related content, etc.

That maps quite nicely onto the mental model that web designers have for the word "footer." The difference is that, whereas we are used to having one footer for an entire document, HTML5 allows us to also have footers within sections.

```
<section>
  <header>
    <h1>DOM Scripting</h1>
  </header>
  <p>The book is aimed at designers »
  rather than programmers.</p>
  <footer>
    <p>By Jeremy Keith</p>
  </footer>
</section>
```

aside

Just as the header element matches the concept of a masthead, the aside element matches the concept of a sidebar. When I say "sidebar," I'm not referring to position. Just because some content appears to the left or to the right of the main content isn't enough reason to use the aside element. Once again, it's the content that matters, not the position.

The aside element should be used for tangentially related content. If you have a chunk of content that you consider to be separate from the main content, then the aside element is probably the right container for it. Ask yourself if the content within an aside could be removed without reducing the meaning of the main content of the document or section.

Pullquotes are a good example of tangentially related content; they're nice to have, but you can remove them without affecting the comprehension of the main content.

Remember, just because your visual design calls for some content to appear in a sidebar doesn't necessarily mean that aside is the correct containing element. It's quite common, for example, to place an author bio in a sidebar. That kind of data is best suited to the footer element—the specification explicitly mentions authorship information as being suitable for footers (FIG 5.01).

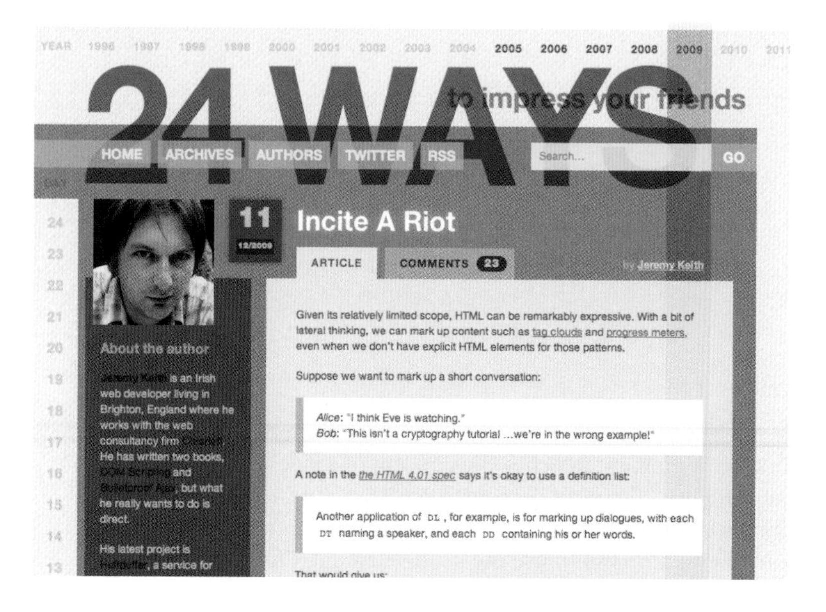

FIG 5.01: The "about the author" text in this screenshot should be marked up with footer, not aside.

Ninety percent of the time, headers will be positioned at the top of your content, footers will be positioned at the end of your content, and asides will be positioned to one side. But don't get complacent. Stay on your toes and watch out for the remaining ten percent.

nav

The nav element does exactly what you think it does. It contains navigation information, usually a list of links.

Actually, I'd better clarify that. The nav element is intended for major navigation information. Just because a group of links are grouped together in a list isn't enough reason to use the nav element. Site-wide navigation, on the other hand, almost certainly belongs in a nav element.

Quite often, a nav element will appear within a header element. That makes sense when you consider that the header element can be used for "navigational aids."

article

It's helpful to think of header, footer, nav, and aside as being specialized forms of the section element. A section is a generic chunk of related content, while headers, footers, navs, and asides are chunks of *specific* kinds of related content.

The article element is another specialized kind of section. Use it for self-contained related content. Now the tricky part is deciding what constitutes "self-contained."

Ask yourself if you would syndicate the content in an RSS or Atom feed. If the content still makes sense in that context, then article is probably the right element to use. In fact, the article element is specifically designed for syndication.

If you use a time element within an article, you can add an optional pubdate Boolean attribute to indicate that it contains the date of publication:

```
<article>
  <header>
    <h1>DOM Scripting review</h1>
  </header>
  <p>A small lighthouse for what has been a long »
  and sometimes dark voyage for JavaScript.</p>
  <footer>
```

```
      <p>Published
        <time datetime="2005-10-08T15:13" pubdate>
        3:13pm on October 8th, 2005
        </time>
      by Glenn Jones</p>
    </footer>
  </article>
```

If you have more than one `time` element within an article, only one of them can have the `pubdate` attribute.

The `article` element is useful for blog posts, news stories, comments, reviews, and forum posts. It covers exactly the same use cases as the hAtom microformat.

The HTML5 specification goes further than that. It also declares that the `article` element should be used for self-contained widgets: stock tickers, calculators, clocks, weather widgets, and the like. Now the `article` element is trying to cover the same use cases as Microsoft's Web Slices (http://bkaprt.com/html5/8).[3]

It seems very unintuitive to me that an element named "article" should apply to the construct known as "widget." Then again, both articles and widgets are self-contained syndicatable kinds of content.

What's more problematic is that `article` and `section` are so very similar. All that separates them is the word "self-contained." Deciding which element to use would be easy if there were some hard and fast rules. Instead, it's a matter of interpretation. You can have multiple articles within a section, you can have multiple sections within an article, you can nest sections within sections and articles within articles. It's up to you to decide which element is the most semantically appropriate in any given situation.

3. The long URL: http://www.ieaddons.com/en/webslices/

A cure for div-itis?

HTML5 gives us the handful of new structural elements described above. They're especially handy if you're putting together a conventional site, such as a blog. Most blog designs consist of a header followed by a series of articles, with some tangential content in an aside, and finished off with a footer (FIG 5.02).

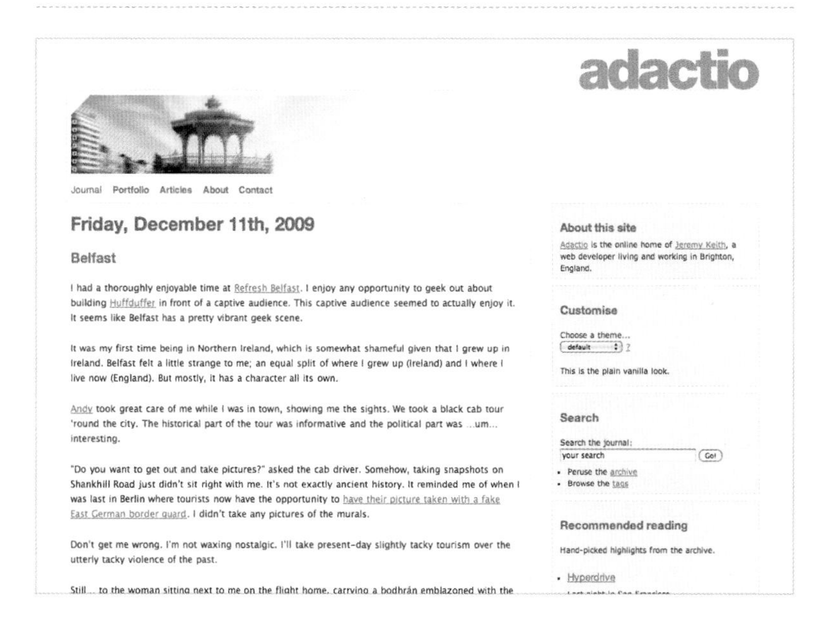

FIG 5.02: The blog of yours truly.

You can now replace some of your `div` elements with more semantically precise structural elements. Don't go overboard, though. Chances are, if you are using a `div` today, you will still be using a `div` tomorrow. Don't swap your `div` elements for shiny new HTML5 elements just for the sake of it. Think about the content.

These new elements weren't created just to replace `div` elements. They provide web browsers with a completely new way of understanding your content.

CONTENT MODELS

Previous flavors of markup divided elements into two categories: inline and block. HTML5 uses a more fine-grained approach, dividing elements into a wider range of categories.

Inline elements now have a content model of "text-level semantics." Many block level elements now fall under the banner of "grouping content": paragraphs, list items, divs, and so on. Forms have their own separate content model. Images, audio, video, and canvas are all "embedded content." The new structural elements introduce a completely new content model called "sectioning content."

Sectioning content

It's possible to create an outline of an HTML document using the heading elements, `h1` to `h6`. Take a look at this markup, for example:

```
<h1>An Event Apart</h1>
<h2>Cities</h2>
<p>Join us in these cities in 2010.</p>
<h3>Seattle</h3>
<p>Follow the yellow brick road to the emerald city.</p>
<h3>Boston</h3>
<p>That's Beantown to its friends.</p>
<h3>Minneapolis</h3>
<p>It's so <em>nice</em>.</p>
<small>Accommodation not provided.</small>
```

That gives us this outline:

- An Event Apart
    - Cities
        - Seattle
        - Boston
        - Minneapolis

This works well enough. Any content that follows a heading element is presumed to be associated with that heading.

Now look at the final `small` element. That should be associated with the entire document. But a browser has no way of knowing that. There's no way of knowing that the `small` element shouldn't fall under the heading "Minneapolis."

The new sectioning content in HTML5 allows you to explicitly demarcate the start and the end of related content:

```
<h1>An Event Apart</h1>
<section>
  <header>
    <h2>Cities</h2>
  </header>
  <p>Join us in these cities in 2010.</p>
  <h3>Seattle</h3>
  <p>Follow the yellow brick road.</p>
  <h3>Boston</h3>
  <p>That's Beantown to its friends.</p>
  <h3>Minneapolis</h3>
  <p>It's so <em>nice</em>.</p>
</section>
<small>Accommodation not provided.</small>
```

Now it's clear that the `small` element falls under the heading "An Event Apart" rather than "Minneapolis."

I can subdivide this content even further, placing each city in its own section:

```
<h1>An Event Apart</h1>
<section>
  <header>
    <h2>Cities</h2>
  </header>
  <p>Join us in these cities in 2010.</p>
  <section>
    <header>
      <h3>Seattle</h3>
    </header>
    <p>Follow the yellow brick road.</p>
  </section>
  <section>
    <header>
      <h3>Boston</h3>
    </header>
    <p>That's Beantown to its friends.</p>
  </section>
  <section>
    <header>
      <h3>Minneapolis</h3>
    </header>
    <p>It's so <em>nice</em>.</p>
  </section>
</section>
<small>Accommodation not provided.</small>
```

That still gives us the same outline:

- An Event Apart
  - Cities
    - Seattle
    - Boston
    - Minneapolis

The outline algorithm

So far, the new sectioning content isn't giving us much more than what we could do with previous versions of HTML. Here's the kicker: In HTML5, each piece of sectioning content has its own self-contained outline. That means you don't have to keep track of what heading level you should be using—you can just start from h1 each time:

```
<h1>An Event Apart</h1>
<section>
  <header>
    <h1>Cities</h1>
  </header>
  <p>Join us in these cities in 2010.</p>
  <section>
    <header>
      <h1>Seattle</h1>
    </header>
    <p>Follow the yellow brick road.</p>
  </section>
  <section>
    <header>
      <h1>Boston</h1>
    </header>
    <p>That's Beantown to its friends.</p>
  </section>
  <section>
    <header>
      <h1>Minneapolis</h1>
    </header>
    <p>It's so <em>nice</em>.</p>
  </section>
</section>
<small>Accommodation not provided.</small>
```

In previous versions of HTML, this would have produced an inaccurate outline:

- An Event Apart
- Cities
- Seattle
- Boston
- Minneapolis

In HTML5, the outline is accurate:

- An Event Apart
  - Cities
    - Seattle
    - Boston
    - Minneapolis

hgroup

There are times when you might want to use a heading element but you don't want its contents to appear in the document outline. The hgroup element allows you to do just that:

```
<hgroup>
  <h1>An Event Apart</h1>
  <h2>For people who make websites</h2>
</hgroup>
```

In this case, the level two heading "For people who make websites" is really a tagline. In an hgroup element, only the first heading will contribute to the outline. The first heading doesn't necessarily have to be an h1:

```
<hgroup>
  <h3>DOM Scripting</h3>
  <h4>Web Design with JavaScript »
  and the Document Object Model</h4>
</hgroup>
```

Sectioning roots

Some elements are invisible to the generated outline. In other words, it doesn't matter how many headings you use within these elements, they won't appear in the document's outline.

The `blockquote`, `fieldset`, and `td` elements are all immune to the outline algorithm. These elements are called "sectioning roots"—not to be confused with sectioning content.

Portability

Because each piece of sectioning content generates its own outline, you can now get far more heading levels than simply `h1` to `h6`. There is no limit to how deep your heading levels can go. More importantly, you can start to think about your content in a truly modular way.

Suppose I have a blog post entitled "Cheese sandwich." Before HTML5, I would need to know the context of the blog post in order to decide which heading level to use for the title of the post. If the post is on the front page, then it appears after an `h1` element containing the title of my blog:

```
<h1>My awesome blog</h1>
<h2><a href="cheese.html">Cheese sandwich</a></h2>
<p>My cat ate a cheese sandwich.</p>
```

But if I'm publishing the blog post on its own page, then I want the title of the blog post to be a level one heading:

```
<h1>Cheese sandwich</h1>
<p>My cat ate a cheese sandwich.</p>
```

In HTML5, I don't have to worry about which heading level to use. I just need to use sectioning content—an `article` element in this case:

```
<article>
  <h1>Cheese sandwich</h1>
  <p>My cat ate a cheese sandwich.</p>
</article>
```

Now the content is truly portable. It doesn't matter whether it's appearing on its own page or on the home page:

```
<h1>My awesome blog</h1>
<article>
  <h1>Cheese sandwich</h1>
  <p>My cat ate a cheese sandwich.</p>
</article>
```

HTML5's new outline algorithm produces the correct result:

- My awesome blog
    - Cheese sandwich

Scoped styles

The fact that each piece of sectioning content has its own outline makes it the perfect match for Ajax. Yet again, HTML5 displays its provenance as a specification for web applications.

Trying to port a piece of content from one document into another introduces some problems. The CSS rules being applied to the parent document will also apply to the inserted content. That's currently one of the challenges in distributing widgets on the web.

HTML5 offers a solution to this problem in the shape of the `scoped` attribute, which can be applied to a `style` element. Any styles declared within that `style` element will only be applied to the containing sectioning content:

```
<h1>My awesome blog</h1>
<article>
  <style scoped>
    h1 { font-size: 75% }
  </style>
  <h1>Cheese sandwich</h1>
  <p>My cat ate a cheese sandwich.</p>
</article>
```

In that example, only the second h1 element will have a font-size value of 75%. That's the theory anyway. No browsers support the scoped attribute yet.

Therein lies the rub. Before you can start using a new addition to HTML5, you need to consider the browser support for that feature. I have a few strategies to help you get started with HTML5, no matter what the browser support is like. In the next and final chapter, I'd like to share those strategies with you.

6 USING HTML5 TODAY

IF YOU WANT TO START using HTML5's new structural elements today, there's nothing stopping you. Most browsers will allow you to style the new elements. It's not that browsers actively support these elements, it's just that most browsers allow you to use and style any element you care to invent.

STYLING

Browsers won't apply any default styling to the new elements. So, at the very least, you will want to declare that the new structural elements should force a line break:

```
section, article, header, footer, nav, aside, hgroup {
  display: block;
}
```

That's enough for most browsers. Internet Explorer has special needs. It resolutely refuses to recognize the new elements unless an exemplar of each element is first created with JavaScript, like this:

```
document.createElement('section');
```

JavaScript genius Remy Sharp has written a handy little script that generates all of the new HTML5 elements. Load this script within a conditional comment so that it's only served up to the needy Internet Explorer:

```
<!--[if IE]>
  <script src= »
  "http://html5shiv.googlecode.com/svn/trunk/html5.js">
  </script>
<![endif]-->
```

Now you can style the new elements to your heart's content.

Headings

Browsers haven't yet begun to support HTML5's new outline algorithm but you can still start using the extra heading levels available to you.

Geoffrey Sneddon has written a handy online tool that will generate an outline as specified in HTML5 (http://bkaprt.com/html5/9).[1]

If you follow the advice in the HTML5 specification and start afresh from `h1` within each piece of sectioning content, your CSS rules could get very complicated very quickly:

```
h1 {
  font-size: 2.4em;
}
```

1. The long URL: http://gsnedders.html5.org/outliner

```
h2,
section h1, article h1, aside h1 {
  font-size: 1.8em;
}
h3,
section h2, article h2, aside h2,
section section h1, section article h1, section aside h1,
article section h1, article article h1, article aside h1,
aside section h1, aside article h1, aside aside h1  {
  font-size: 1.6em;
}
```

That's just the first three levels and it doesn't even cover all the possible combinations of headings within sectioning content.

Fortunately, the HTML5 outline algorithm is pretty flexible. If you want to use heading levels the old-fashioned way, that won't affect the outline in any way.

ARIA

The new structural elements in HTML5 will be very useful to assistive technology. Instead of creating "skip navigation" links, all we need to do is use the nav element correctly. This will allow screen reader users to skip past navigation without us having to provide an explicit link.

That's the plan, anyway. For now, we must make do with the technologies that browsers and screen readers support today.

Luckily for us, there is currently excellent support for ARIA (Accessible Rich Internet Applications).

At its most advanced, ARIA allows assistive technology to participate fully in all-singing, all-dancing Ajax interactions. At its simplest, ARIA allows us to specify even more semantic richness in our documents.

The most basic ARIA unit is the `role` attribute. You can add `role="search"` to your search form, `role="banner"` to your masthead, and `role="contentinfo"` to your page footer. There's a full list of values in the ARIA specification at http://bkaprt.com/html5/10.[2]

You can also use these role values in HTML 4.01, XHTML 1.0, or any other flavor of markup, but then your document will no longer validate—unless you create a custom doctype, which is a world of pain.

But ARIA roles are part of the HTML5 specification so you can have your ARIA cake and validate it.

You can also use the added semantics of the `role` attribute as styling hooks. The attribute selector is your friend. Selectors like these allow you to distinguish the headers and footers of a document from the headers and footers within sectioning content:

```
header[role="banner"] { }
footer[role="contentinfo"] { }
```

VALIDATION

Used wisely, a validator is a very powerful tool for a web designer. Used unwisely, a validator provides smug nerds with an easy way of pointing and laughing at other people's markup.

Henri Sivonen has created a full-featured HTML5 validator at http://validator.nu/.

You don't even need to update your bookmarks pointing to the W3C validator (http://validator.w3.org/). That too uses Henri's parser as soon as it detects the HTML5 doctype.

2. The long URL: http://www.w3.org/TR/wai-aria/roles#role_definitions

FEATURE DETECTION

If you want to start using some of the more advanced input types in HTML5, you'll need a way of testing for browser support so that you can provide JavaScript alternatives.

Modernizr is a useful JavaScript file that will detect support for input types as well as `audio`, `video`, and `canvas` (http://www.modernizr.com/).

The script creates an object in JavaScript called Modernizr. By querying the properties of this object, you can determine whether the browser supports a particular input type or not:

```
if (!Modernizr.inputtypes.color) {
  // JavaScript fallback goes here.
}
```

Modernizr will also perform the sleight of hand that allows you to style the new structural elements in Internet Explorer—so if you use Modernizr, you don't need to use Remy's script as well.

CHOOSE YOUR STRATEGY

It's entirely up to you how ambitious or cautious you want to be with HTML5.

At the very least, you can take your existing HTML or XHTML documents and update the doctype to:

```
<!DOCTYPE html>
```

You have just taken your first step into a larger world. Now you might as well start using ARIA roles as well; what have you got to lose?

If you're nervous about using the new structural elements, you can still get used to the new semantics by using class names as training wheels:

```
<div class="section">
  <div class="header">
    <h1>Hello world!</h1>
  </div><!-- /.header -->
</div><!-- /.section -->
```

Further down the road, when you're feeling more confident about using new HTML5 elements, you can replace those `div` elements and class names with the corresponding structural elements.

While it might still be too early to use some of the more advanced input types such as `date`, `range`, and `color`, there's no harm in using `search`, `url`, `email` and other simple input types. Remember, browsers that don't recognize these values will simply treat the input as if it were `type="text"`.

If you're feeling adventurous, you can start playing around with `audio`, `video`, and `canvas`. They might not be ready for prime time, but they could be fun toys to experiment with on your personal site.

Resources

I often write about HTML5 on my personal site:
http://adactio.com/journal/tag/html5

I'm not the only who's excited about HTML5. The mighty Bruce Lawson is also jotting down his thoughts:
http://brucelawson.co.uk/category/html5/

Bruce is just one of the contributors to HTML5 Doctor, an excellent community resource packed with great articles:
http://html5doctor.com/

If you fancy getting into the more complex side of HTML5, Remy Sharp is pushing the boundaries: http://html5demos.com/

Mark Pilgrim has written an exhaustive book called *Dive Into HTML5*. Buy it from O'Reilly or read it online: http://diveintohtml5.org/

For those occasions when you need to go straight to the source, keep the HTML5 specification on speed dial: http://whatwg.org/html5

The HTML5 specification includes a lot of information intended for browser makers. The W3C hosts an up-to-date version of the specification specifically for authors: http://www.w3.org/TR/html-markup

GET INVOLVED

As you embark on your adventure in HTML5, you may find parts of the specification confusing. That's okay. It's more than okay; it's very valuable feedback.

There are some very smart people working on HTML5, but web designers are under-represented. Your perspective would be greatly appreciated.

You can join the HTML Working Group at the W3C as a public invited expert—ignoring the Kafkaesque language of an invitation you need to issue to yourself—but I wouldn't recommend it. The associated mailing list has a very high volume of traffic, most of it related to politics and procedure.

The WHATWG mailing list is the place to go if you actually want to discuss the HTML5 specification: http://www.whatwg.org/mailing-list#specs

There's also an IRC channel. Sometimes you want to go where everybody knows your handle: irc://irc.freenode.org/whatwg

Don't be shy. The IRC channel is a great place to ask questions and get answers from Ian Hickson, Anne van Kesteren, Lachlan Hunt, and other WHATWG members.

THE FUTURE

I hope that this little sashay 'round HTML5 has encouraged you to start exploring this very exciting technology. I also hope that you will bring the fruits of your exploration back to the WHATWG.

HTML is the most important tool a web designer can wield. Without markup, the web wouldn't exist. I find it remarkable and wonderful that *anybody* can contribute to the evolution of this most vital of technologies. Every time you create a website, you are contributing to the shared cultural heritage of the human race. In choosing HTML5, you are also contributing to the future.

INDEX

ABOUT A BOOK APART

Web design is about multi-disciplinary mastery and laser focus, and that's the thinking behind our new line of brief books for people who make websites.

A Book Apart publishes highly detailed and meticulously edited examinations of single topics. We are pleased to launch our new publishing venture with Jeremy Keith's *HTML5 for Web Designers.*

COLOPHON

The text is set in FF Yoga and its companion, FF Yoga Sans, both by Xavier Dupré. Headlines and cover are set in Titling Gothic by David Berlow, code excerpts in Consolas by Lucas de Groot.

ABOUT THE AUTHOR

Jeremy Keith is an Irish web developer living in Brighton, England, where he works with the web consultancy firm Clearleft. He has written two previous books, *DOM Scripting* and *Bulletproof Ajax*, but what he really wants to do is direct. His online home is adactio.com and his latest project is Huffduffer, a service for creating podcasts of found sounds. When he's not making websites, Jeremy plays bouzouki in the band Salter Cane. His loony bun is fine benny lava.